Timmy's Story:

A Story About Autism and Friendship!

For more information, please email Tim at: tips4inclusion2018@gmail.com

IBSN: 978-0-578-84070-3

This book is dedicated to all the children with autism and other disabilities.

Written, illustrated and published by, Timothy Rohrer creator of Tips4Inclusion

Edited by Amy Rohrer

Graphic designer: Anthony San Philips

"May you never have to struggle fitting in like I did as a child!"

Timothy Rohrer

Timmy is a cute boy
who is funny and smart
but does not have any friends.
There are things that
make him different from
the rest of the kids in his
neighborhood and at school.

When Timmy's mom asks him a question, he does not answer her. He is more focused on playing with his toy race car and superhero.

Timmy has obsessions with his toys. He talks about them at his house, at school and everywhere he goes.

Talking in complete sentences is very difficult for Timmy. He likes to only talk about his race car and superhero repeatedly which seems to make him feel better.

Whenever Timmy hears dance music, he will flap his hands and jump which is something called stimming. He often does this when he becomes excited. (Stimming makes him calm down and feel better.)

Touch is very difficult for Timmy. He gets scared whenever his mom touches his shoulder.

When Timmy hears fire alarms, he cries, screams and covers his ears. The noises of the fire alarm are too loud for him.

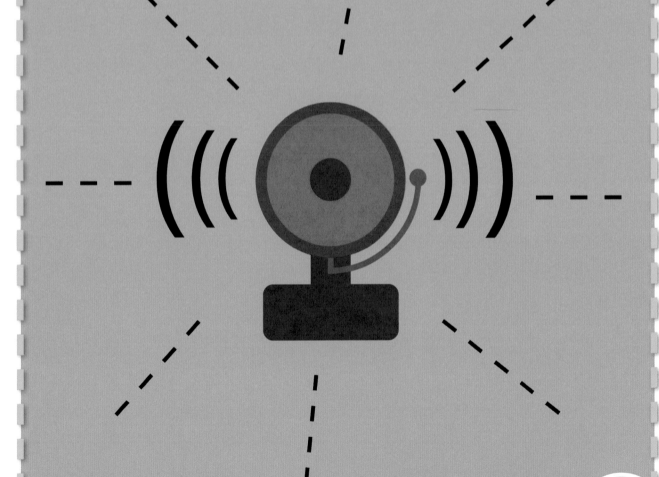

One day, his mom decided to take him to see a doctor and talk about all the things that make Timmy different. The doctor said Timmy has a condition called autism which alters the way one communicates and reacts to the world around them.

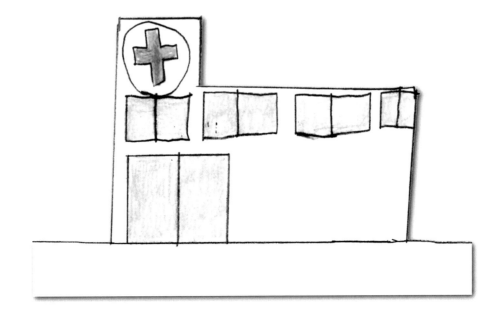

Timmy's mom was happy to learn he has autism because now she could find ways to help him.
She made an appointment with a speech therapist to help teach him how to communicate.
Ms. Karen talked about animals, sports and other things besides his racecar and superhero to get him used to other subjects.

Ms. Karen suggested that they buy sensory toys. Timmy and his mom then drove to the store to buy a sensory brush, slime and a whistle. (These toys are supposed to help children with autism overcome their fear of touch and noises.) After dinner each night, Timmy uses the brush on his skin for ten minutes and then plays with his slime.

Thanks to the toys they bought, Timmy feels much better whenever his mom taps his shoulder. Blowing the whistle helps him adjust to the noise of the fire alarm however, he is still scared when they go off at school.

Timmy's mom felt she needed to talk with his teacher, Ms. Bethany about his autism and the things that make him different. She was concerned that he does not have any friends. Ms. Bethany was wonderful and wanted to teach the class about autism and how to be friends with someone with a disability.

Ms. Bethany had a talk with the kids about what it is like to be Timmy. She explained his obsessions and communication difficulties. She also mentioned that Timmy does not like the noises of the fire alarm and uses sensory toys to help him with things like sound and touch. However, she told the kids Timmy also likes art, music and recess just like any other kid. The kids learned that being different didn't mean they couldn't all be friends.

The kids in Timmy's class went home that day and asked their families more about autism. They were so excited to learn more about Timmy and why he was different. More importantly, the kids wanted to try to make friends with Timmy and include him more in class and in playdates.

Timmy became much happier in school and at home because he was included in more activities and invited to playdates and places like the park, movies, and bowling.

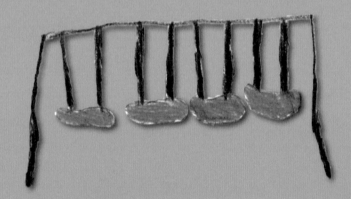

For more information, please email Tim at:
tips4inclusion2018@gmail.com

To find out more about Tim's Educational Resources, please visit:
https://tips4inclusion.wixsite.com/disabilityinclusion

Made in United States
Orlando, FL
23 March 2022

16081769R20020